ARCTIC BUGS

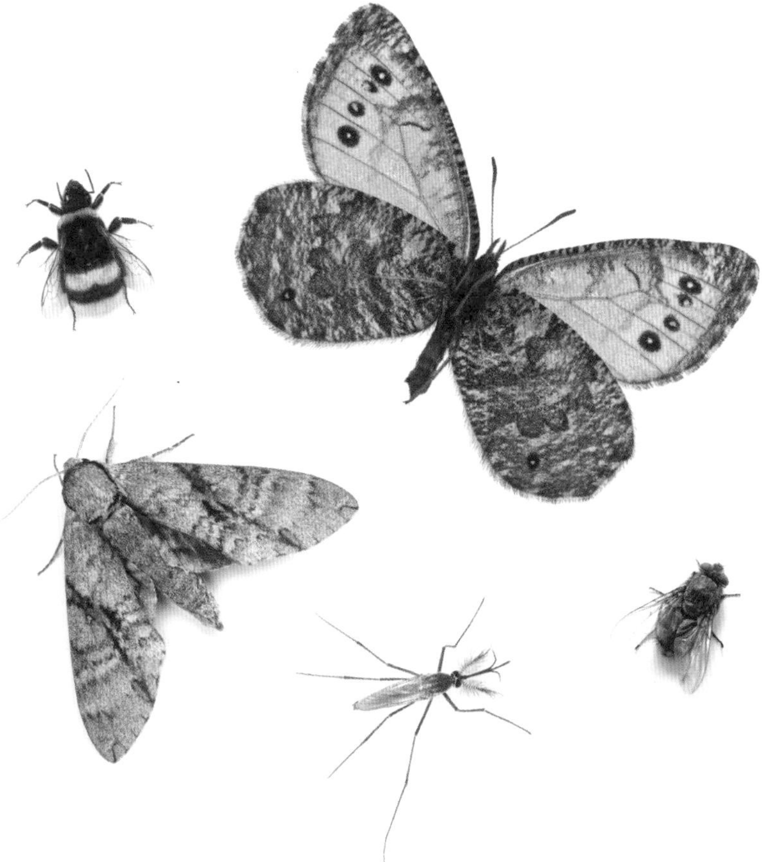

This is a beetle.

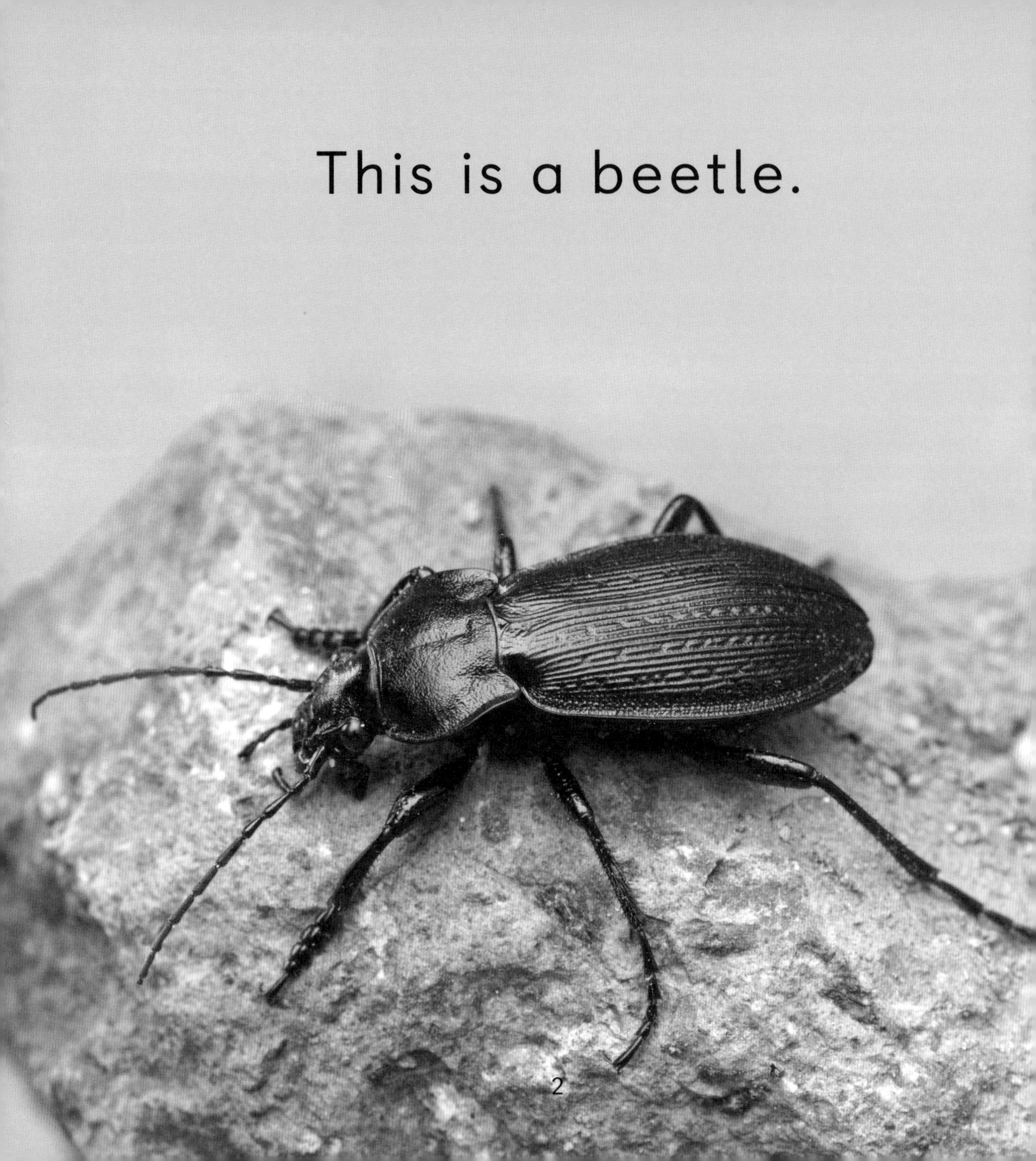

This is a fly.

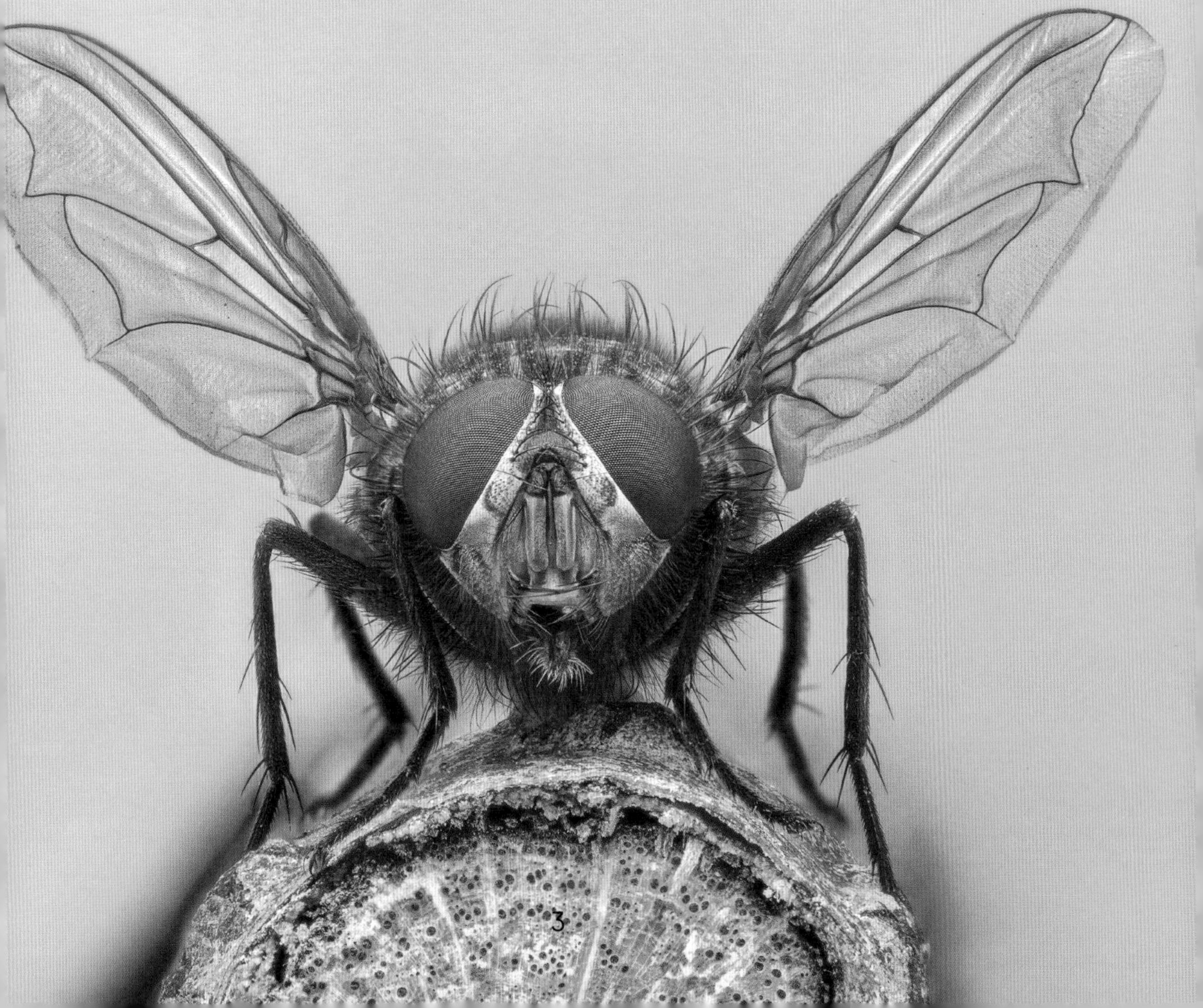

This is a mosquito.

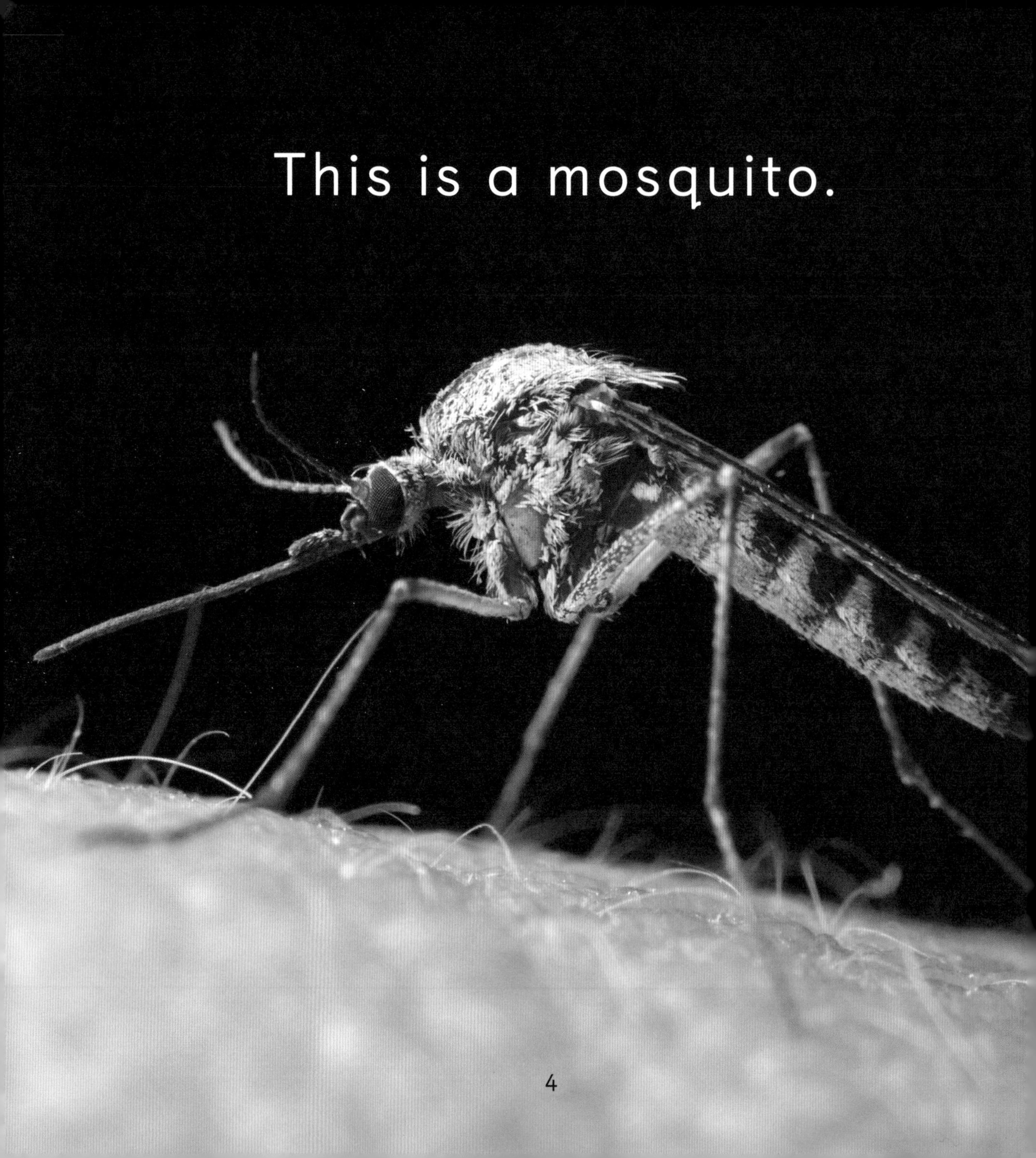

This is an Arctic bumblebee.

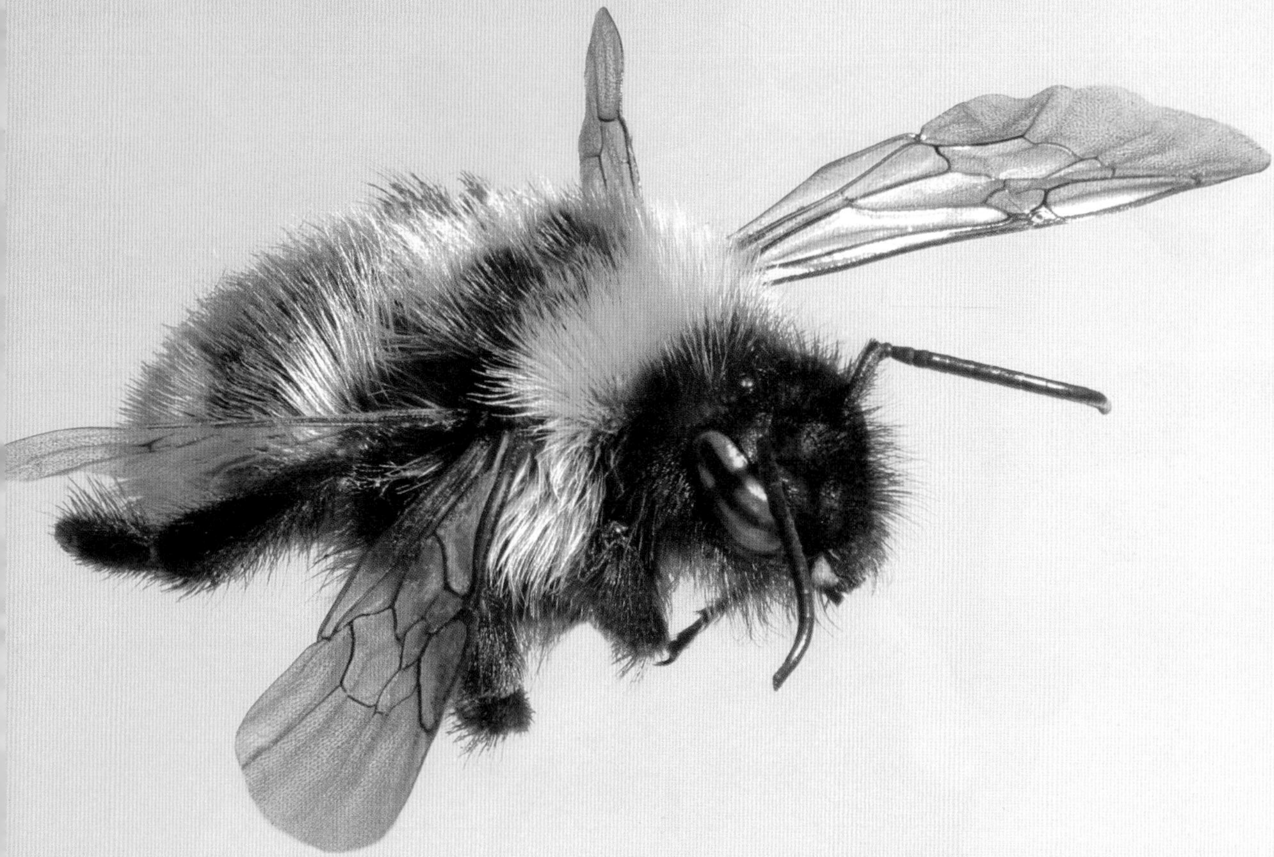

This is a butterfly.

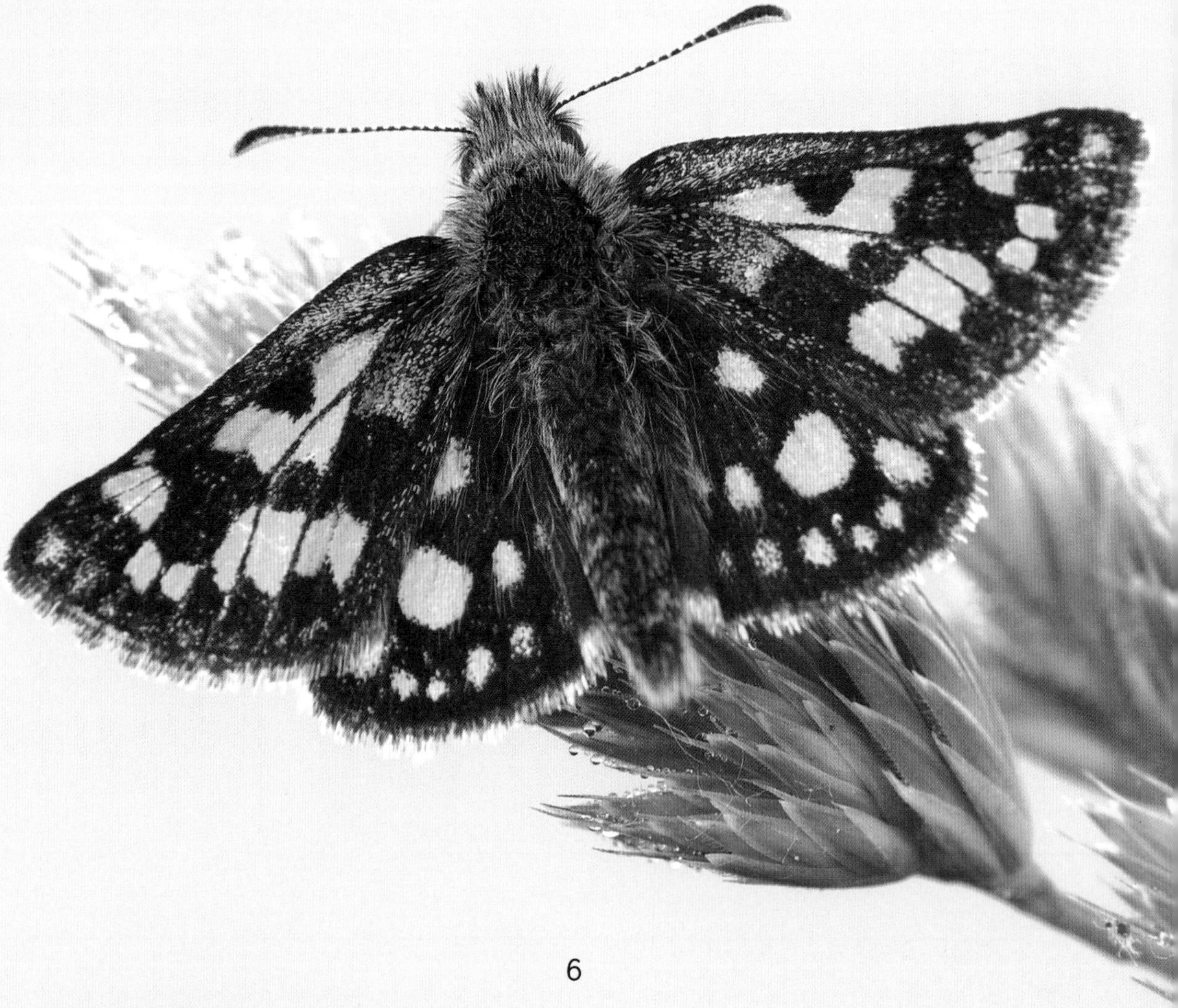

This is a moth.

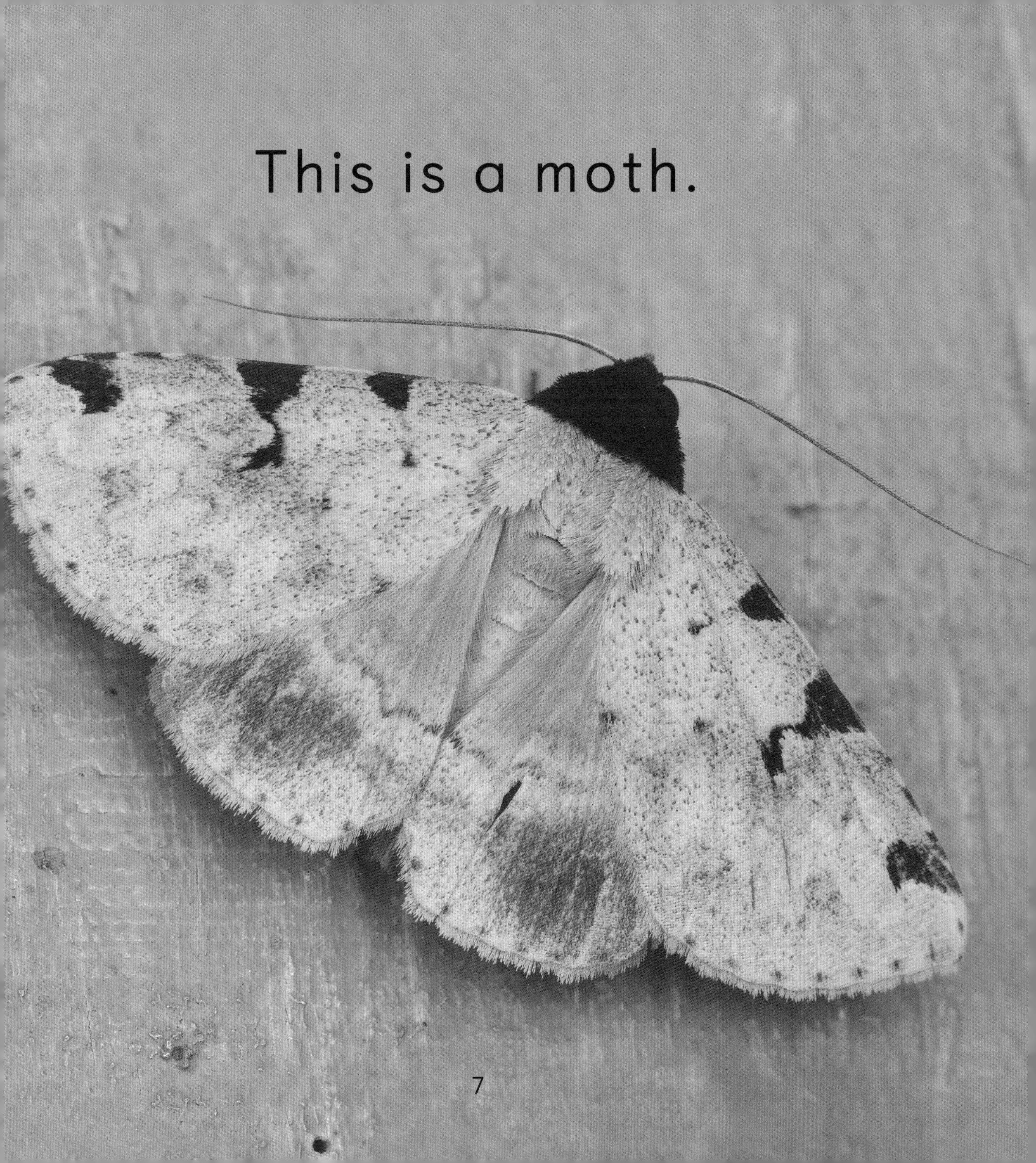

This is a wolf spider.

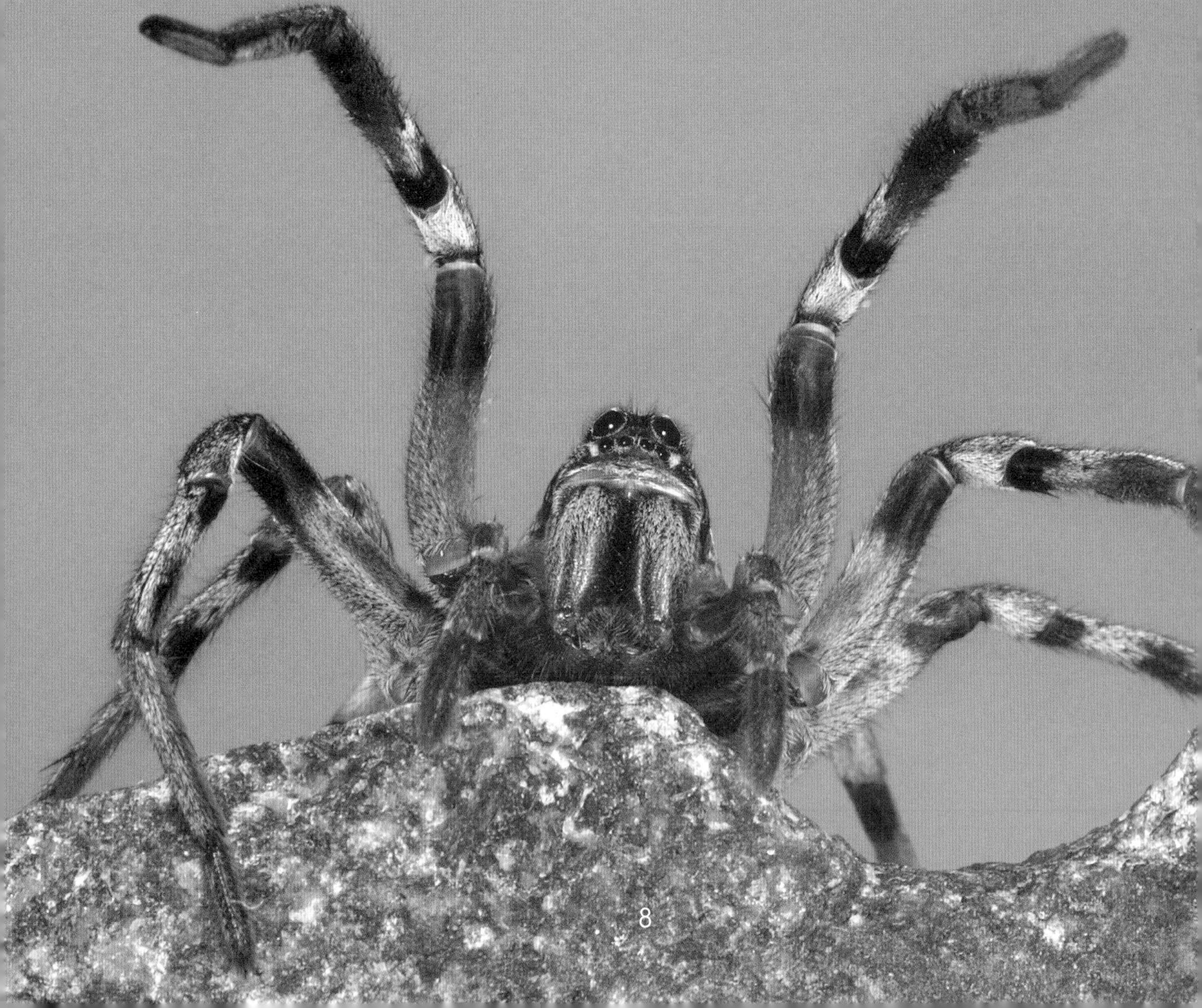